A Human Saloon

Poems by R. Nikolas Macioci

Kung Fu Treachery Press
Rancho Cucamonga, CA

Copyright © R. Nikolas Macioci, 2019
First Edition 1 3 5 7 9 10 8 6 4 2
ISBN: 978-1-950380-54-1
LCCN: 2019947867

Design, edits and layout: Jason Ryberg
Cover and title page images: Jon Lee Grafton
Author photo: R. Nikolas Macioci
All rights reserved. No part of this publication may be reproduced or transmitted in any form or by any means, electronic or mechanical, including photocopying, recording or by info retrieval system, without prior written permission from the author.

To my best friend, Sandra Feen,
with much love and gratitude for
traveling the tumultuous road with me

TABLE OF CONTENTS

A Human Saloon / 1
Transition / 2
Strangers Pray at Night / 5
Dancer / 6
Articulated Memoir / 7
Exordium Introduction To an Intimate Discourse / 8
Prelude / 9
Sacraments / 10
Autumn Mistake / 12
An Earlly Outing / 14
A Rundown Life / 15
Lecture to Someone From the Streets / 17
Invisible Relationship / 18
The Myth of Intimacy / 19
Ambivalent Lover / 21
Self-Persuasion / 22
Say No / 23
What Really Happened In a Photograph
   of Spring Trees / 24
If Only / 25
Sunday in the Present and Past Tense / 27
The Constant Criminal / 28
Residence / 29
Realization / 30
Asexual / 31
Assessing Second Chances / 32
December Afternoon / 33

Helpless Prey / 35
It Matters Briefly / 37
September Leaves / 39
Defeat / 40
Lies / 42
Survival / 43
Entering Maryhaven / 44
Wretched Memoirs, Graceless Love / 45
Rain and Recovery / 47
A Moment of Morning / 48
Again / 50
Vagrancy / 51
The Velvet Cage / 53
Fury / 54
Portrait of Discovery / 57
Entering the House at the Wrong Time / 59
Winter Upon My Happiness / 60
The Passionate Room / 62
The Town Where the Marvelous Never Happened / 63
Departure / 65
King of Unacceptable / 66
User / 68
Inconclusive Resolve / 70
Lesson in Despair / 72
Voice of Autumn Vacancy / 74
Omen / 75
The Button / 77

Lyric / 78

Finished / 80

Relinquishment / 82

The Ghost of Old Love Comes Back On Sunday / 83

Personal Confetti / 85

Beginning and Conclusion / 86

Aftermath / 88

The Progression of Letting Go / 89

Finale / 90

The Act of Leaving / 91

The Final Act of Leaving / 92

Damned By the Decision / 94

Lamenting Loss / 95

The Reality of Retrospection / 96

Conclusion / 97

Empty Streets / 98

Epilogue / 100

A Human Saloon

I

*..believe in a love that is being stored up for you
like an inheritance...*

-Rainer Maria Rilke, *Letters to a Young Poet*

A HUMAN SALOON

You give me a thumbs up from across the
barroom because I have hit the slots. My
hand rises to return the signal. *Buy
you a drink?* you ask, sliding your body
up next to mine as if the simple key
to end solitude were contact of thigh
against thigh. It is in our minds to try
intimacy, to become the trustee
of each other's loneliness. We agree
to a one-night stand that leads to four years
of repetitious arguments which part
us in negative ways we could not see.
Our empty end of romance summons tears
and anger translatable into Art.

TRANSITION

The leftover part of Aunt Liz that hadn't succumbed
to Alzheimer's died on a rainy Friday night
at Grant Hospital. Sitting beside her bed, I
released her hand, letting go of twenty years
of caregiving. I shut her eyes and, as if in someone
else's body, descended stairs to my car.

I drove without destination, listening to windshield
wipers slide back and forth and the swish of tires
spinning off water. And then at a traffic light
I began a half-laugh, not because of anything
funny but because I'd just been freed from the
gritty loneliness of tending to my aunt's disease
single-handedly.

Wipers continued to slash rain as I pulled into
the first bar I'd been in since Aunt Liz became
sick. I ordered a beer and took a seat in the corner
at a slot machine. The fifth pull on the handle
spun three red sevens into view, and I turned
and gave a thumbs up toward the bar. One
person from the crowd signaled back then
walked my way. We talked cliches and began
to like each other enough to remove our clothes
at my house.

The relationship lasted three and a half years,
enough time to explore a jungle of woes and
to seek freedom again.

That rainy October night when my aunt died,
I stepped into wrong love without guilt, removed
the shackles of caregiver that I had worn for years
like a threadbare jacket.

II

It is difficult to know at what moment love begins; it is less difficult to know that it has begun.

-Henry Wadsworth Longfellow

STRANGERS PRAY AT NIGHT

I had nothing to write about and so
slipped on my jacket and drove to a
nearby bar. The place was crowded
with what looked like the forgotten people
of the world. I sat at the slot machine
with a handful of dollars. Three red
sevens settled on the winning line.
I turned toward the bar with a thumbs
up. You returned the signal then edged
towards me. Nothing kept us from
making a poem from the rest of the night.

We braided fingers as if in prayer. There
was a constancy to the ache to lie down
with you, to begin a religious repose
of our bodies. Our ankles were the last
parts of us to touch. Ordination into
the holy pressed us together. There was
righteousness in the ritual discovery
of each other, a spiritual exegesis
of our context.

By morning, I drove you home, stopping
on the way for donuts and coffee. We
blinked under the unforgiving blaze of
fluorescent light like ones who had emerged
from limbo. For the present we believed
in fate, our creed: to assume faith in the
rightful unification of our hands.

DANCER

I stumble onto you through careless dreaming,
place myself on a barstool not because I need
a drink but because I need the person I hope
for to say hello.

Lights dim, and you dance in the middle
of dollar bills. Afterwards, I detain you
and risk a floundering introduction. Walls
flock with shadows, stage lights glare
through colored gels; you stride to your
dressing room.

You reappear, find a stool beside me.
I pay for your drink, and when I lean closer,
I smell sweet cologne. You laugh when I touch
your forehead to shift a stray lock of hair.
Are you up to dance again I ask. You answer no
and moisten your lips with a smile. Then
when I least expect it, I find words
to invite you home. I have never been so bold.

We lie on the bed, drifting toward each other's
warmth, whisper drowsy wishes. We inch
toward romance, weeks later, toward deceptions
stage lights didn't illuminate.

ARTICULATED MEMOIR

You're going to be beautiful naked
when you slide out of your clothes and into
desire, I'll be holding my breath, motionless,
desperate to steal you onto my skin.
Night is a room in our relationship,
and I mean for you to know romance there.
Let me cross the shallow distance between
us, dispose of decorum, bend into slow
kissing, elaborate touching, the blessing
of you constantly in my mind. Come
against me, let me wear your body
as my own. All of my life presses into you
singing the motion of love. Let me be
grateful to God for holding silence of
your soul in my arms.

There is pleasure in creating each other,
and beyond an earthly union, we choose
to lie together afterward with laughter,
with calm proof of compatibility.
I care that you're under my heart, eyes waiting
for that wordless look of happiness.
A streetlight thieves a bit of dark, but we
lull in the length of each other's shadow,
listen to the rare lurch of a late car. Sometimes
I nuzzle your neck, the sum of our peace.

EXORDIUM INTRODUCTION TO AN INTIMATE DISCOURSE

I love to watch you undress.
The first glimpse of your skin in shadowy light
from an adjacent room, the curve of your back
down to your buttocks draws me close, and I
want to touch you with the most delicate touch
my hand can give. And then you move to the
bed and slide onto your back as if posing
for a painting. Fully clothed I lower myself
beside you, kiss your chest with adoration.
In the semi dark we are outlines of love
wanting the first move to be exquisite.
Satisfaction surfaces with a kiss. I lean over
your lips, feeling your warmth through my
shirt. It is the beginning of two bodies
becoming coincidental, forming a single
tenderness.

PRELUDE

As rain falls I touch you, hand lingering
for a decision. You find my hand and
join our fingers with your answer. Your
skin is luminous as summer berries.
I kiss your shoulder, bare now that you have
leisurely removed your clothes. I stay dressed,
unabashed at adoring your body, demonstrating
desire that dares to lie beside you and whisper
submission. You smell of lilac and longing,
and I am ready to release you from hunger.
Rain raps windows like soft pellets. I look
at your perfection, rain-streaked and slightly
shadowed. You pull me to you across your
nakedness, and I'm numb with pleasure. I
love the stretch of you beneath me, long
tapered legs, warmth of your deepest secret
known now against my denim. I savor
the hint of unuttered anticipation, romantic
marks of rain written over both of us.

SACRAMENTS

I'm hungry for your religion, for psalms
of your flesh, for the tongue of communion
from your kiss. Holding your face in my hands
is prayer and church. Baptize me, take me
into the rain with you. Expose me to the
catechismal questions of lovers. Be my
chancellor, my divine flirtation. I will
not doubt the dogma of who you are, the
doctrines you live by. Enter night with me
under light of the ecclesiastical moon.
Let me be your daystar in the morning
when the finger of God points at us
and our great awakening. Let me lie
in the arms of your divine grace. We will
decimate your demons with the gospel
of our relationship, bathe each other
in the holy water of happiness. I will sing
the hymn of my devotion to you, again
and again.

III

Secrets are festeriing parasites to a relationship, devoring their hosts from within, leaving behind a empty husk of what once was.

-Mark W. Boyer, Devlyn Lycurg,
Book one: Prelude into Darkness

AUTUMN MISTAKE

This is the day I learned that your heart
is a field of weeds from which I bent
to pick a wildflower when none was there.

Sun flickers silver of a wheel rim across
the windshield. I want us to explore the
country of autumn, its explosion of color,
but first I have to know where you have
gone, leaving only a shadow of yourself
beside me as we travel along route 56.

Your head leans against the side window
as if you planned to sleep through the
rest of your hopeless life.

I nudge you and say, *Look.* Sugar maples
orange as tigers. Katsura trees blazing
scarlet and yellow. You move, still asleep.

For a couple of hours I drive with enormous
appreciation for leaves painted in the madness
of psychedelic colors.

At a roadside park, you step outside,
uninterested in scenery, still dazed from
what I suspect is a drug fix.

At this rest spot, I follow a path through
the trees while you slump on a bench
and turbulent creek water roars beside me.

AN EARLY OUTING

You are a pseudo astronomer
who looks up at noiseless stars whenever
you are far enough away from city trees
to see their white light.

At this point you are between lives, friends
with criminals, a criminal yourself, yet
someone who claims to want to live as
pure as love.

On this night we go for a ride, stop by a
farm field and at its edge, see stars flare
above ebony. Words seem empty as you
look up and find Orion and Aries. A
bird startles from undergrowth. Still, we
look up, and you tell me about your
estranged daughter. There is so much
communication for that second, and then
you stop, say you are a loser, and
infinite silence becomes as impenetrable
as the stars. Your body shines bright
with starlight, your face free of failure.

I drive you home over the Scioto River,
a sorrowful song on the radio sounds
miles away. When you get out, I watch
you walk away under streetlight, knowing
your life will come to nothing.

A RUNDOWN LIFE

Rent money due and not a coin in his pocket,
he peers at the mirror, dabs himself with
borrowed cologne. His Jordans were a gift.

At thirty-three he grips the excuse of bad
background for his criminal charges. In
desperation he decides to dance at a
neighborhood bar.

Lights focus on a small raised platform.
Fully clothed he hops onto the stage to
"Big Things Poppin." His hip hop moves
flow from locks to breaks, to boogaloos.

He strips off clothing one piece at a time
until he's in skimpy underwear. The bar,
crowded as ringside at a prize fight, cheers,
shouts, yells in approbation. Many stuff
bills into his waistband.

He exits off stage and behind a makeshift
curtain, counts his money: twenty dollars
in tips not counting the sixty dollars he
will be paid for performing.

On the street he lights a cigarette, coughs, bums a ride home from a customer. He's due in court the next morning for violating a warrant. Writing bad checks caught up with him.

He crawls into bed feeling defeated, pulls the blanket with cigarette holes up to his neck like a comforting hand.

LECTURE TO SOMEONE FROM THE STREETS

Have you found a job yet? The last time we talked,
you said you were looking through listings. I don't
understand the jobless upheaval when around
every corner is a *Now Hiring* sign. Like
a lost transient, you've dropped three positions
during the last three years. You yield to defeat
too easily. You dream of, smile at, but murder
chances to coax yourself into a better world.
Your mother fed you pills. Your father killed
himself with heroin. You found him dead
one morning with his head down on the kitchen
table. Are you an exception to your background?
Can you ameliorate your life? You've assimilated
the uniform of your neighborhood: tattoos,
earring, sleeveless t-shirt, pot addiction,
dependence on someone else for your security.
Will you always be part of the majority,
sing the same rap songs, sponge from each
other? Destitution defines your life.
Self-deception explains your character.
Are you capable of more than strip dancing
in a bar and selling Jello shots? Walk
around the corner for another smoke?
Saturate yourself with failure, become toothless
and long haired, hang out at the local bar.

INVISIBLE RELATIONSHIP

Yours was an unknowable heart. When I
looked into it, I saw stone, only the
shadow of a pulse. Of course, it's degree
of love that counts, but I can't dignify
your silence with excuses. I did try
on many occasions to help you see
why always sleeping in the car was key
to unlocking the truth behind your lie,
and then there was your tendency to treat
me as if I were non-existent. At
the end of three years, I caught on to you
and learned about your extensive rap sheet,
drug addiction, and warrant. It was that
chat we never had that turned the day blue.

THE MYTH OF INTIMACY

During winter when trees retained snow that
turned to ice, you lay in my bed,
and I lay behind you, my arm across your
chest, your hand over mine. Both of us
fully clothed, we held that position until
we slept. Throughout the night ice melted,
and by morning, sun monopolized the room.
I moved, and you awakened. Outside
the window, trees dripped like ruined sculptures.
I felt at that moment the power of love
was in our bodies, but you rose and went
into the living room, got a soda
from the refrigerator, and turned on
the television. Something about your silence
told me more than words could have.
I looked at you on the sofa, the soda
on the coffee table. Why wouldn't you
want to be amorous at the opportune time?
You wrestled into your coat, and I drove
you home. At your house we parked and argued
who should have made the first move. Anger
surged like a flash flood. You sprang from the car
and slammed the door. Driving home I recognized
the inevitable had begun, falling away
from each other like opposing magnets. Why?

Who to blame for inertia, for not being willing to connect? At home I looked at the barely mussed bed and thought of Andrew Marvell's "To His Coy Mistress."

AMBIVALENT LOVER

A maniac moon gaping in the big night
overgrows the sky. Insomnia, a poison
to sleep, guides me to the window. The
yard is an island edged by chain link fence.
In the glass my face says young, but I know
I exist as old as fire, feel wrinkles of
my skin with a subtle hand.

I watch staggering clouds astride the moon,
riding it like a jealous cowboy. Aluminum
stars break open with brightness.

I hand myself a life of cowardice. How
many times a day have I learned to love
you in the shadow of words, but against
the wall I will not name you. Truth is
blacked out for the sake of family. They
think I deserve the dogs of hell. My
innocence is obsolete.

At the window I am starlit, rectitude
of the heart challenged by lies. The
mocking stars have figured out my
oppression. I stand at the window
wanting to hold you with my tangled
emotions, to tell you that I forgive
myself for always returning to guilt.

SELF-PERSUASION

I want to crave you again with three
small words, but you've been a creature
of neglect, and I back away while there
is still a peaceful separation.

It's a blessing for both of us to think
about beginning again, to break from
old habits, start something new that
this time might be forever. It's admittedly
burdensome to back off from established
practices of mind and body, the familiar.

It's autumn. The beginning of melancholy
makes us want to return to times that
might have been moments ago or years
past when happiness seemed possible.

I'm staring at light on pond water in Schiller
Park, watching the absence of your reflection.
Confident geese wonder whose hand they
will feed from next. In your abject poverty,
you also puzzle over the possibility of
another meal.

It is drug habits your parents introduced
you to during your teens that strain our
relationship. I have temporarily slipped out
of it, closeted my passion because recently
I found more contentment in being alone.

SAY NO

How to walk away from the knife point
of caring when everyone but you knows
it's madness to remain in a relationship
because of routine.

You lay down faults like placemats
on the kitchen table on which I put two
cups of coffee and grievances. I provided
a cargo hold full of possibilities to grant
excuses for drug abuse, joblessness, and theft.
You capsized justification, flailed in spurious
self-defense. I swam away from an
unsuccessful rescue, but I did go back over
the water looking for bones, for any reminder
of what I wanted from you in the first place.

You who are reading this are right in thinking
me fresh from an asylum for re-exposing
myself to a ruined relationship.

Everywhere I look, answers surface, but none
are within reason. None hold the logs of
common sense together the way dog lines
secure a raft.

I forgive myself for what I dared to pursue,
for performing like a clown with a broken smile.

WHAT REALLY HAPPENED IN A PHOTOGRAPH OF SPRING TREES

Four flowering cherry trees stand side by side.
Their blossomed branches fan upward like
the tail of a Leucistic peacock, white against
a Pacific blue sky. A single boy waits beneath
the trees for a bus.

I park my car on a side street, sling my camera
strap over a shoulder and head toward the trees.

In my lens they are a panorama, a spring corridor
of interlocking blooms. I amble beneath them
for an angled close up. I compose another shot
looking straight up as if under a popcorn white
umbrella.

It feels as if thousands of blossoms are wasted,
as if I know that these photos will mean less
without you in them. I think it is time to accept
that your absence is permanent.

The boy boards the bus, and it roars away. I
start toward the car, stop, glance back, wondering
if the need to love you is still in my eyes.

IF ONLY...

If only I could lock your arms around me
in lasting trust, turn the pages of the past
until they disappeared.

If only you could lead me away from the
person you are to the one you aspire to be.

If only I loved you fifty percent less than
my two hundred percent investment.

If only your habit of wearing black were for
my appreciation and not for an anonymous
audience, and you were an accredited
author of the heart for the pages of my life
you've already written on.

If only I were not someone on the sidelines
whom you infrequently acknowledged.

If only you sang songs to me you saved
for others. I would cup my hands around
your face and bring our lives together
to show you something beyond the temporary
infatuation of first appearances.

IV

Like a driver who has lost control, I was bracing for the impending crash.

-Zack Love, Stories and Scripts: an Anthology, Worst Valentine's Day Ever: a Short Story

SUNDAY IN THE PRESENT AND PAST TENSE

Nostalgia dictates late mid-summer
afternoon through the window
above my desk. I observe oak trees,
their leaves unmoving as a worn out
memory. Malcontent, I mellow
and allow myself to recall a scene

of us leaning on the bridge railing
watching white ducks make frivolous turns
in the water. I enticed the ducks
to shore as if to feed them. They turned
and swam away when they saw I had
no food. I always thought it would be
you who strayed, but I drifted to finality
to save myself from your reckless course.
The ducks went on swimming as if I weren't there.

You went on, and I'm at my desk
on a Sunday, finding you in my heart
again, your eyes, your voice, the voyage.
The trees have mostly disappeared in dusk.
Their shadowy branches hold nothing
more than sleeping birds and twilight.

THE CONSTANT CRIMINAL

You knock at my door, after
many days of waiting. Tangled emotions
wondered if I'd ever see your face
again. I feel a dryness in my throat.

Memory glides to guilt that I begrudge you
another chance, but I grapple with your
ghetto existence, glamor of guns, grazing in
pastures of drugs, running with floaters and
convicted felons. I halfway believe you're
angry with your past, want out of it
like a dirty piece of clothing. I cannot
stop the howl inside my heart, the
sound of your breath next to my ear as you
sleep. I almost want what I fear; to be
a part of your downward slide.

Don't, in fact, knock again at my door. Think of
us as a ruined rose, wilted from attempting
to grow in the wrong season. I tried to stop
your human erosion, break you free of a
perpetual cycle of defeat.

You light the next cigarette.

RESIDENCE

You won't open your front door to let me in.
The lock unlatches and you stand there
blocking the way. What riches are you hiding
in your house? Heroin? Cocaine? Marijuana?

Bed sheets, substituted for curtains, pull back
an inch, and a curious eye peeks out. I am
apprehensive about what I will discover.

How many drug dealers come and go in a
day, wearing their low-slung wrong doing
below their beltline? What are their badges
and passwords for entry besides a smoking
cigarette and profanity? Are you part of
the goings on or just providing the premises?

I'm not an aristocrat, nobleman, or a peer,
but our roots are too different to be part of
the same tree. You startle from sleep at the
sound of gunshots. I awaken staring at a
branch of white dogwood blossoms.
Little by little the contrasts have begun
to divide us.

How do you live in a world where debris and
crumpled hearts accumulate along the curb?

REALIZATION

You are as desirable as a gardener in the spring.
I want to compliment your face, but reluctance,
like sweat, crawls down the branches of my spine.

You go into the kitchen, looking for a glass.
I stay seated, or rather don't move, which is
puzzling because I think I hear you leave through
the back door. Outside, you strike a match in a
mortar joint of the house, inhale a night-glowing
gulp of marijuana.

I am careful with you on the patio, because
the whole evening seems at risk. I hate
that I don't want you now, that I want to clear
the air of you.

You know nothing of real life, nothing of bees,
soft flowers, and leaves. I hate you now for
embracing me with nothing but sexual temptation
and a glimpse of your addiction.

I will remain chronically alone while your
affection for drugs turns my back toward you.
My mouth forms goodbye. I hear you singing
tears, but what good are they when you are
steeped in a double life of dependency?

ASEXUAL

How disillusioning to go to passion's depth
and find empty compromise. Your whereabouts
is questionable even when you're present.
Where were you when I was willing
to worship your mediocrity, wrap myself
around neutral feelings? Worst was withholding
whole moments of yourself when it seemed
as if your body refused to participate.
You exuded ennui. You were even exempt
from listlessness, inert, unmoving, immobile.
A mannequin would have marshaled more
emotion. We never figuratively merged.
You methodically manipulated me into
believing we were matched. I ministered
to a subdued model of narcissism.
Masquerade did not mirror out mismatch.
Our moral truth unmissable: You lay inward,
your body astonished by its needs. I
devoured everything within the corridors
of desire. These days I don't know your
whereabouts. You may still be wondering
in limbo, arms at your sides, lying
mummified as if murdered, waiting for
the next mouth to come down on yours
without you having to change position
or budge. You are not the creature I am
dreaming of, the rousing answer to loneliness.

ASSESSING SECOND CHANCES

My hands are so cold that a fist is a
ball of ice. All warmth draws out of
me into this poem.

Late December afternoon throws a
reluctant sunshine against the window.
I blow on a hot cup of tea. Islands of
snow top dormant brown grasses. I
wait hundreds of years to hear from
you, and when I do, everything I've
forced away will come back. A
storm of thoughts twist into a knot.

In my imagination, we heave
like broken boats, fight the downward
pull of defeat, sinking. Gulls bark in
the sky, look for the living or the dead,
make circles above a vortex at the bottom
of which we make a watery grave of our
relationship.

Gulls drip defeat from talons,
hover with persistent eyes. I look out
a window at the bay, see nothing better
than bright sailboats on which you pad
barefoot, trimmed in blue sky, and in
spite of what we've lost, reach for me too.

DECEMBER AFTERNOON

Maybe I will go to Schiller Park alone
and occasionally stand off to the side
wondering about cruelty and the mistake
I made in allowing it. It will be cold
like blades in the blood. Delicate
birds will rush from bare branches to
warm electrical wires, but sun will soothe
the shell of memory that is filled with acts
of deceit. You threw away

my trust like a winter coat no longer in
fashion. You snorted lies. You stole
from me in the darkness of my own home,
crushed and rubbed out a joint on the bricks
of my parents' house leaving another black
mark on our relationship.

The pond will be frozen and especially
smooth enough to see my face in the part
skaters have not roughed up. They will
be scripting figure eights and etching
circles. The best skaters will spin and
maybe fall in an attempt to add beauty
to routine moves.

Maybe I will stay home by the fireplace
and listen to logs popping out sparks.
Maybe then I will settle in this room,
shut my eyes, and let loving you fall
onto the logs like a willing sacrifice
to the god of freedom.

HELPLESS PREY

I have pity for the hophead, his dim eyes
and dirty fingernails, the dark secrets
he refuses to tell. With a match he strikes
black marks in the mortar joints of my house,
inhales a high from marijuana .

Who reads his agony in the black marks
that bleed down the bricks? Who soothes
his slumped shoulders, blurts out his dreams
for him?

I have seen days when soberness trickles
through his veins like weeping, and he promises
to thank God for his precious loneliness
and jump from the whorehouse of wasted life
into withdrawal.

He has learned to smell the police from blocks
away, to leap fences, stride nonchalant through
a poor man's neighborhood undetected.

I once saw him caught and searched. Cops
cuffed and threw him into the backseat of
a cruiser.

All year he lives in a winter room of hell,
scrambles for bread, carries a knife in his
pocket, threatens to die by his own hand,
hangs with all the wrong friends.

On his best days, he speaks of detoxification,
doctors shutting him away for two weeks,
drowning him in sobriety.

IT MATTERS BRIEFLY

Whose love have I been prisoner to?
Someone who strikes me as the wellhead
of insincere words, who mumbles slang
and looks drawn and peaked from an intake
of street drugs.

You took a last look at sky before turning
your face toward the mindless high of heroin
and entered the boarded-up existence of
addiction.

Now I speak of what is left of us, turn on
a lamp and write a testament to loss that
lies in the pit of my stomach like poison
berries.

I am aware of your delicate sickness that
no amount of affection can heal.

After two bypass surgeries, I have an
obligation to my heart's health that has
at its center a hole you cut with the dull
edge of a paring knife.

I am aware of your slow death, the
second-rate self that is not good enough
to pity. I am raw with anger that after
shelling out hours of hope you ended us
with drug-directed journeys along back
streets and alleys brooding with suspicious
shadows.

This is said to you without hearing what
you have to say because who can bear more
lies when only weeping waits to enter
the front door of my mind?

SEPTEMBER LEAVES

You were as lean as a long-distance walker
last time I saw you, shadows of lush lashes
on cheeks, short coffee-brown hair,
eyes green as chrysoprase.

You looped your arm in mine, and we meandered
through Schiller Park in late afternoon.
Mid-September sycamore leaves had begun
to cover the sidewalk like yellow stepping
stones, air as crisp as toast.

I felt an elegant passion for you,
a sophisticated closeness, the kind
of bond other people recognize.

Even then, I suspected we were wandering
toward a kind of darkness, instant decay.

That day in the park proved rare. Penny
wishes in the pond didn't prevent
the surfacing of your criminal past.

I pushed the knife of finality into both
of us, turned it until my hands were bloody
with conviction you would never change.

DEFEAT

You never held me like you wanted me.
I think of darkness in a room where
branches made shadows on curtains.
All summer I attempted to lift away
emptiness between us, lash your demons,
pin mine to the wall like donkey tails.

Your body fascinated me, and I tried
to curve into it to show intimacy, but
we weren't paddling on the same river.

You used to slam doors because I quibbled
with your logic. Once, you hurtled a
basket of clean laundry across the lawn
when I cornered you in a lie. Mutual
trust snapped in half like a fragile stick.

I hoped for a solid connection, a
companion who understands the imminence
of death and forsakes the petty.

There was never that silky passion as
your spine bent over my humble body.
I looked up at you, and your eyes were dull.
You never looked at me.

I can't say anything more except the
mystery of love was hidden from us.
You saw nothing wrong with your neglect game,
making me wait until midnight for a stoic
embrace, streets below us desolate as you
turned away.

LIES

I insist that you use the truth with me
the same as you would training an animal.
Do not steal my grief for truths you wouldn't
accept. It would take Christ to restore your
sincerity.

We have manipulated each other's love.
We are, in that sense, murderers, and no
man has the right to take away another
man's defeat or dying or make amusing
comments about the love he has to give.

I saw you once walking under the trees
in Columbus, and you made a display
of friendliness, clean as concern but
rotten and empty as old roots. You have
infected my life with kindness while
whispering guilty in my ear for a past
I buried. Because I hear you, I listen
to stones falling off your tongue. Leave
me without hope for nothing in your arms
is comforting.

I am an old man every day I forgive you
for nothing. When the door of hell flies open,
I will be safe from the lonely earth and
from curses you banished me with.

SURVIVAL

You are headlong away from me now.
I will not continue to fill your pockets
with money. I've loosened the chains
of love, saved my own life from
being crushed under wheels of neglect.

How could I have so willingly given
up my existence for yours? You are
locked in decay. Once a guiltless child,
you suffered parents who, like perverse
magicians, made your conscienceness
disappear with cocaine and pills.

Sometimes I want to offer you my life
in exchange for the tatters of yours, but
I feel numb in the offering and would,
instead, urge you to slug the past in the
jaw with two fists, black out the abuse
that was your parents' incarnate. Stop

the blight of your childhood from
touching you anymore. Find holiness
in yourself. Shout, *I'm done.* Go
back to school. Become serious about
surviving, want the power to abdicate
the throne of wretched poverty. Even
without a bridge, it's time to cross the
river.

ENTERING MARYHAVEN

Pulling your suitcase behind you,
your loneliness blinded me as I cared
about your disappearance behind doors
of detoxification.

A little boy whose parents passed chemicals
to him, whose Dad lay his head down on the
kitchen table and died of an overdose of heroin
has challenged the horror of recovery.

It's a long autumn afternoon. The sun sinks
down, but still there's light. From the outside
I stare at the cold wing of rooms, wondering
which room is yours. Tomorrow I will bring
you dollar bills to use in the vending machines.

You vowed to stay and not walk out unclean.
I breath easier now that you have surrendered
your habit to people who can help.

You didn't look back at me, but I know you
understood without a backward glance that
I hadn't abandoned you. I am ready for you
to live your life, but you must first get it back.

I turned and hummed a classical tune, happy
for your new and delicate beginning, but my
shoulders sagged because it was a hell of a
way to say goodbye.

WRETCHED MEMOIRS, GRACELESS LOVE

I write about your four year effort to master
duplicity, call it love. Each lie, a
water drop, dripped into a stalactite of mistrust
that hung from the roof of my mind until the
day it would break loose, spear my gut with
hurtful astonishment. Another water
drop would form. Another stalactite.

Even in Schiller Park beneath white blossoms
of mock cherry I wanted to bellow how you
had distorted my life into a funhouse mirror
that even I didn't recognize. I should have
abandoned you early on to the drugs you cared
more about than any human love. Actually,

I left you many times, but returned because
of your words I was fool enough to believe.
Your lies became as common as window
glass. You didn't drive, so I hauled you
around and wore blinders in those alleys
where drug dealers dwelled in shadowy houses
behind drawn curtains.

Back home, no amount of washing cleansed
the stealth and underbelly of those nights from my
mind. Again and again you exposed me to risk

for the sake of bliss that lifted you higher than
birds fly and left your head pressed into sleep
against the car's side window. I was more alone
with you than when you weren't physically there.

The last time I saw you, you had entered a
treatment facility, and I bolted the door
of our relationship behind you. There was
nothing left of us but dust and twisted memories.
I walked away from you, and it almost hurt, almost.

RAIN AND RECOVERY

The last day of October, a scrap of month
left, rain strums city like a string
instrument.

I am cold, slumped inward at the dining
room window, watching trees flick off last
leaves.

Have I mentioned the kind of life that hides
in my words? When I write, whatever I write
is for you.

Through liquefied glass I stare at squirrels
on the edge of the lawn. Rain streams through me.
I shiver as if running a finger over the jagged edge
of a tin can. I need to tell you how your absence
rips my heart. Someday you will come from detox,
push open the door on a new life. Now, your are
busy with personal hope, letting the useless
aftermath of drugs out of your veins, learning
to lash out at old triggers.

Squirrels curve their heads into the birdbath,
ignorant of their own reflections. They
simply drink from the cracked basin without
concern for fixing what is broken.

A MOMENT OF MORNING

Is it possible to look into a mirror
and not feel a knife stab the ego?
It is morning, and I apply shaving
cream. Sun creeps up over a side
window, gold as a chalice. The
aftershave lotion I apply smells
faintly of pine.

Retired, I have the whole day to stir
through stacks of poems that need revised,
to grow weary of the rainy forecast.

In the kitchen I dump pills from the pill case
into a pile on the counter. A glass
of cold milk suffices. Clouds drift
into view. Later I will listen to rain
slant against the roof and maybe write
a poem.

Somehow, I start the day listless,
lift a key from a hook inside a cupboard
and walk outside to the shed.

The lock is resistant, needs a shot
of WD40. Inside, the door opening

allows only minimum light. I have
stored a friend's lifelong belongings
here, a favor when he went into rehab.
Two storage boxes, tools, and a lawn mower
define his material existence.

The door swings everything shut into darkness.
I open the door and follow a path of lemon sun
back to the house, thinking sometimes
a friendship doesn't last beyond favors.

AGAIN

I'm not pleased that I heard from you tonight.
Your text contained a *Hey* and nothing more.
I guess I knew that this moment was sure
to happen, that I would have to hold tight
to a resolve not to respond. Your plight
is criminal, and I suspect that your
arrest warrant is still active. You roar
excuses: a bad environment, quite
undone by poverty, parent abuse.
I cared for you until you told a lie,
and lying became habitual, so
did your deep entanglement in drug use.
At the end of three years, I didn't try
to change you anymore and let you go.

VAGRANCY

On 4th street laughter is never heard
after dark, and in daylight it comes
from the corner of a mouth, an uplifted
lip, a snarl.

Windows and doors of houses are boarded
with plywood, and you live in such a house.
Your hand is always out, dirty fingernails
bitten ragged reaching toward the properly
dressed for a few bucks.

Your front yard yells dirt and weeds, ditched
cigarette butts. You have descended to
poverty, a derelict in a cycle of self-defeat.

Porches and corners draw midnight gangs,
conjure crime. I told you to look for beauty
elsewhere, that it would always die in your
neighborhood, but I'm afraid that you were
born to walk asphalt in the South End, never
looking your age until insidious ruin steals
your youth.

More criminal than Cane, you kill your body
with drugs, play it off as temporary. You
practiced re-hab for a while, then paid for
heroin with your rent money.

You won't change. Bundle your clothes, climb into the next ramshackle relationship with a stranger under an overpass,   In truth, you aren't worth more than that.

THE VELVET CAGE

My annoyance with your half-closed eyes
led me to suspect that you were injecting
lightening into your veins. I ached to see
your room, to look at the evidence myself.

Your dresser glittered with hypodermic
syringes. Like miniature bicycle spokes
they lay or pointed in every configuration
of disarray. I asked you where you had
punctured yourself. Your answered, *Fingers,
hands, arms, legs, torso.* I felt tipsy from
disbelief that you had made a voodoo doll
of yourself in exchange for short-lived
euphoria, sealed a pact with hell to feel
satin existence, to become a captive
in a velvet cage. You showed me a blotchy
red area on your stomach, a reminder of
where you'd pushed a needle. You revealed
a hundred-dollar-a-day habit that had
sunk you to the bottom. That day, I turned
slightly away from you, unable to stop staring
at the dresser of needles that stared back
like dozens of silver porcupines.

I slumped to my car, turned on loud music,
something that would interrupt seeing the
shadow of pinholes you had become, a
man who had decorated himself with addiction.

FURY

Walk beside me. My language is goodbye.
You have worrying to do. I can't be
silent anymore. What were you this time,
on the edge of addiction or completely
strung out? I do not celebrate what I write
down, nor your misery. I must have been
wounded by loneliness to let you dig a hole
so deep it buried both of us.

You have drained my pockets, used my
dollars for God knows what. It is impossible
to believe that I ever thought we belonged
together. Now, I want to live unloved.

What happened to me in that saloon-ridden
night has morphed into a small hell. I got
nothing from it but to meet your addle-headed
friends, shoulder to shoulder with drug pushers
and users.

At this point I feel as if I'm picking myself up
off the street, trying to remember who I was
before I drove down Frebis Avenue to the
Holy Bird Bar and damned myself
by meeting you.

I am standing at the grave of us, notebook in hand, scribbling details I don't want to forget. My lungs are crazy with rain, but I go on scribbling. I don't want to forget.

V

I went to your site that day to...
I guess to double check

I thought... maybe your wrote
something, a new story... a

message...anything

I did find a new story...

It wasn't about us...

And I ended up feeling even
emptier.

-Stjepan Sejic, Sunstone, Vol. 5

PORTRAIT OF DISCOVERY

I've often wondered what sexual betrayal
would feel like. Now I know. It's a
continuous chill that ripples down
the chest, a shot of novacane in the brain
that freezes on an image of you in your
underwear standing next to a bed in
which she presses under covers to disappear
as I open the bedroom door.

You hadn't expected my visit, and you
left your front door accidentally unlocked.
Many knocks announcing myself to no avail,
I turned the knob. From beneath the
closed bedroom door, a path of yellow
light poured in my direction. With
my hand on the knob I wanted to flee
from what I suspected I would find.
My interest in the outside world stopped,
my focus narrow as deception. And there
you stood, forever in my dumb-struck
mind, your face shouting surprise. I
turned from the yellow light, absolutely
wounded, raced out the door to my car.

Fifteen minutes later I pass cars
on the freeway I didn't see, blinded
by abandonment. I grip
the steering wheel as if strangling
secrecy. Sunlight on the dashboard
negates what's left.

ENTERING HIS HOUSE AT THE WRONG TIME

I drift back to your intolerable lie,
quite remember the teenage girl
in your bed who claimed to stay in
the same room where the only space
heater afforded warmth. She'd been
thrown out of her house. You felt sorry
for her. You stood by the side of the bed
in your underwear, quick to dress when
I opened the bedroom door. A moment
of empty explanation urged disbelief,
and I turned and fled down the hall.

Early morning men in hardhats watched me
weaken into my car, blindly attack
the road home. I wanted to vomit, disgorge
disbelief, but I didn't stop until I dragged myself
from the car that seemed to find its own way
into my garage. I sat silently, giving
myself a second guess about what I'd seen.
My body seemed to be on the seat beside me,
numb and stupefied. I walked deep into
the back of the house to the study and sagged
into a rocking chair, pushed back and forth
my foolish trust.

WINTER UPON MY HAPPINESS

You are winter. Icicles of heroin hang
from your house. On this morning I open
the gray curtains of your life and see someone
else looking back at me from your bed.

There is no advantage to your high
when you have to come back down
to the south end of existence. Your
loving words have vanished from my
heart. I sweep up the dust of our
relationship from the floor of your
ramshackle house.

I have opened your bedroom door on
the startled eyes of a 16-year-old. I
turn away from your conspicuous guilt.
When did you abandon yourself to
oblivion? When did you give up
innocence for the momentary
nakedness of pleasure? With snow on
my hands I shall wash away what I have
seen behind your unbolted door.

All direction is lost as I flee from your
impervious glare. The ridge of day is
turning brighter with dawn, and I hear

nothing but the ragged wash of blood in my ears, the beating of a pulse chasing itself around and around in my head. Our bond is broken, and I will not live long enough to repair it. I am not the help you need for your addiction, and I must escape from the poisoned dream of us and from the shrewd craftiness of your lies. All that was hidden is now outlandishly visible. I drive away with nails in my tires and all the air around me is dead.

THE PASSIONATE ROOM

My mind struggles with an obsessive dance
of imagination that sees your infidelity
bobbing over another person's loins. That day
I opened the door on your bedroom you
stood beside the bed in which you had
satisfied sexual longing. Shock surrounded
me like a roomful of fingers pointing
at my foolish trust. I rushed from the house,
each step a small death, an emotional anchor
weighing my heart to the depth of betrayal.'

I drove home as if under water, oblivious
of landmarks and familiar scenery. Cars
passed me in slow motion. My limbs felt
heavy, injected with anguish. Anger
bloomed in me like a poisonous plant,
its leaves murdering reason. I entered
the garage, shut off the engine, and sat
still, numb with disenchantment.

Weeks later as I stare into soft firelight
and my brain picks the lock on memory,
I realize that I'm a prisoner of that room
and that I've never left it.

THE TOWN WHERE THE MARVELOUS NEVER HAPPENED

I bought you a Chicago Bulls' jacket
and a tousle cap to match. I led you
into numerous stores, purchased
unspeakable numbers of tennis shoes,
shirts, socks, damaged my bank account
in an effort to compensate for disastrous
background when your mom offered you
pill addiction and your dad died before
your eyes of a heroin overdose at the
kitchen table. I understood your damage,
hoped to draw you away from the vortex
of bad habits.

I've turned away from you countless times
after finding an underage girl in your bed,
after finding a photo of you and yet another
girl holding blankets in front of your naked
chests, after failing to tell me you'd been fired
for stealing from Bob Evans' restaurant,
after discovering you had ferreted out
the drug pusher when you worked at
Burger King.

The list of deceptions and lies grew
like a garden of weeds, out of hand
and ugly, but I stayed, believing
you were someone I could save from
Southend habits, from walking alleys
to wrangle a drug deal. You continue
to travel alleys, dodging police, but
I have admitted defeat and turned back
to my world where night is once again
a place of brilliant stars, where choices
would hold up in a court of law, where
the words said to me are true and trusted.

DEPARTURE

I invented the love I had for you
and gritted my teeth when you denounced
it by a heavy reliance on drugs. I say
invented because I made up the
relationship that you were only
marginal in. Our partnership became
a joke because you died every day.
The company you kept, heavily reliant
on heroin, changed my life when I
accidentally opened the door to your
house one morning and found them
naked and in an oblivious cluster. You
stood there holding a blanket up to your
chest. I made a poem from the hurt,
and that is why it doesn't hurt any longer.

Now, you plan to leave Columbus, tricking
yourself into thinking things will be better
in West Virginia. Jobless, drug-addled, your
self-hate is justified. You have been cruel,
deceived me with lies and dishonesty. You
took a hammer to my heart, nailed it to
a thousand deaths. I do not care that you
are urgent for me to talk to you before
you leave town. I welcome your exit,
and after three and a half years of stoic
neglect, I write the best poem yet.

KING OF UNACCEPTABLE

You will never walk by my side again,
or pedal a bike with me through Schiller
Park beneath branches of silver snow, or
stride over hot summer sidewalk toward
the gazebo.

To say your name is a knife in my mouth.
I've managed to slacken our relationship
into nothing more than an empty thought.
Your lies plunged me through the doors
of deceit and the many houses you lived in.
Ramshackle rentals resonated with your
drug deals, revolted me, robbed me of
dignity. Interminably waiting for you
in the car, I had to retool my life to tolerate
your habits. Toward the end, you nullified
all the ethics I'd tried to nurture in you.

You will curl up with your neighborhood
cat, smoke cigarettes the rest of your life,
gaze through a drugged haze each day, hang
out with jailbirds until one of you jumps
in front of a bullet.

You found your niche as a flimflam amateur,
a humdrum pothead. A habitual loser, you're
headed to an all-night diner, decayed teeth,
in debt, needing a haircut, and looking for
a handout. You destroyed us and deserve
only the arms of another derelict.

USER

Drunk on the gold nectar of autumn sun,
I distance myself from dismaying joy,
divorce myself from a glossy dream.

In a chair by the window I think about
our ragged arrangement. You were more than
a friend formed from luminous possibilities,
who forfeited everything for the buzz
in your veins. Your traveled along a stony
road, unsmiling, drove yourself into the
dead end of addiction.

I rise and gaze out the window. Sky is
unmoving. Listening to my own desire,
I think how I've wasted my heart.
I have been trapped in the shambles
of your recovery, ready to vanish from the
vacuum of your vandalized life.
I want to unbind myself from your fevers,
from the sick chaos of your body. I am
utterly weary with no admiration left.

Air in the house is stone heavy. Outside
the day shimmers with thin and delicate
light. I lean against the glass, watch trees

empty their leaves every moment. I listen
to a whispering resolution in my head.
Like the trees, I must divest myself of
what is dead.

INCONCLUSIVE RESOLVE

A workman will soon arrive to replace
the water pump in the basement while I
wait upstairs thinking of suicide. He
can't suspect that I feel as if I've fallen
onto the moon and hit the bottom of a
crater or that I've been plowed under by
a farm tractor that in passing didn't see me.
I have not learned yet how to let go of the
edge of glass. Bloody fingers seem
incidental to retaining the only long-term
partner I've ever had. Getting drunk takes
longer than suicide. There are eight bottles
of beer in the refrigerator. That may be
enough for a bit of oblivion but not enough
for me to let go of unlucky love. I don't trust
death. I fear that if I die, my passion for
you will still be alive, and I will continue
beyond the dusty grave to want another
last day with you. If I could kill passion
and desire, the need for you would vanish.
I could stand at a window and look out at
today's pounding rain and not feel lost. My
life has no pivotal point without you.
It is early April, but the trees are still bare
from the rape of winter. I remember when

leaves turned brown as if their appeal had
been used up, as if they had no other option
but to break from the limbs. The workman
is finished and trudges up the steps. The
edges of his boots crust with old mud.
He is lucky to have something mechanical
to occupy his mind. He must keep his lust
and ardor in his back pocket. I pay him and
he leaves. Did he see pain in my eyes before
he left or suspect the direction in which
my demons are leading me?

LESSONS IN DESPAIR

I never learned how to love an addict,
the secrets, lies, the everyday deceptions
common as breath, yet my heart was
overwhelmed with you, and I longed to
hurl your damaged past.

I watched your mind and body wrestle
with withdrawal, saw you vomit
on the sidewalk, gave you money for
suboxone to tide you over until
you could enter rehab and detox. I learned
through you to be street smart, but I hated
the lessons.

I used to massage your neck, and all
the while my hand caressed your skin, I
wondered what narcotic inched its way through
your veins under my very fingers.

I have a deep guilt for not trying harder
to understand your addiction, but you had
this habit of throwing me left curves, surprises
that chilled my gut and staggered my mind
with disbelief: theft, deception, infidelity.

I found you with another heroin addict
who videoed both of you engaged in sex.
Though sickened by these dark moments,
I tried to keep the door of our relationship open,
but suffered humiliation, didn't speak to you
for days. If I look in a mirror I see a fool who has
my face, breathes my breath, but it is not I.
It is someone who gave himself to my own form
of addiction for you.

I cry out in despair at my failure
to love you more than you loved drugs.

VOICE OF AUTUMN VACANCY

I stroll through Schiller Park and name the trees.
I gaze at paint poured over suicidal leaves.
Rouged and in golden robes they peel to the
pond, slip over the surface like small coffins.

I do not hide my loneliness. It's as conspicuous
as a woman's purse. I awoke today and wondered
who loved me. I'll awaken tomorrow and wonder
the same thing.

I listen to birds sunning themselves, to the cough
of a passerby walking his dog. What brought me
here is everything I look at, the knife of late sun
slicing between limbs, the white silk of a swan's
feathers, the precious patience of parents with
children.

I want nobody else, but I don't want to be alone.
I am happy for other people to know me, and I
promise to take care of friends, but, oh, I can
live without you.

Twilight the color of egg yolks and flamingos
plunders the sky. Crickets have begun their
essay on night. I open the car door. The street
lights edge out darkness, pave a path of
ponderous shadows. Cyclists pass me in twos.
I start the engine, escape from being marooned
by melancholy.

OMEN

I awaken, feel irregular
palpitations, the fatal flutter of
the final days of our relationship.

I could go on being hooked by your plush
skin, the scent of your cologne or toss
open my heart and shoo out its dark warning.
I am soaked, as if by rain, by the dozen drops
of consideration that forestall a decision.

I believe it is best if we walk away
from each other. When we examine
our lives, we find only sorrowful
incompatibility. Your poverty rich background
has siphoned the broth of life from me.
You have ignored my deepest meaning
as a poet, taken dollars from my pocket
with and without my permission.

What is the reason we try to love?
At this point I can settle for failure.
There are only so many chances
in this world, and I have given them
all to you, twice.

If someone is always saved by someone else,
in a different life it might have been us. You
are the fox in *The Little Prince,* and I have
mistakenly tamed you, an egregious error,
an exceptionally bad choice.
The black butterfly lifts its wings,
enters my heart for a final time.

THE BUTTON

How lame of me to block your phone calls
when each day you're the first person I want
to hear from.

Today I relented and unblocked you.
We can listen to each other say farewell
or head back to a better beginning. This
time I haven't protected myself with
misgivings. I'm open to your spurious
explanations, ready to talk about
addiction to methadone, sexual betrayal.
I will listen to your tears of supplication
ask me for help with groceries, utility bills,
rent. I will give you money as I have
many times before, but I will resent
that you follow the path of a vagrant.
I cannot sleep when hard times overwhelm
you, but I cannot protect you beyond reason.

My finger is poised again above the button.
A late winter afternoon mellowed me.
In truth, I need to press it again
and finalize good-bye.

LYRIC

This is the way I forget about you.
The boredom of unmemorable drives
when you were asleep against the window.
I take out my pen, drowsy as I am,
and write away all the bad memories.
This is the way I forget about you.

This is the way I forget about you.
Your habit of making me wait too long
while you sucked on a cigarette elsewhere.
The lies that kept me fishing for the truth
when you had, in fact, been fired from your job.
Words I put down give me welcome distance.
This is the way I forget about you.

This is the way I forget about you.
Pot addiction you would not confess to,
stubbing your joint on the side of my house.
Jobless but always asking for money.
My purge is from the pen. Make no mistake.
This is the way I forget about you.

VI

A sad thing in life if that sometimes you meet someone who means a lot to you only to find out in the end that it was never bound to be and you just have to let go.

-Dave Mathews Band

Maybe the most that you can expect from a relationshio that goes bad is to come out of it with a few good songs.

-Mariane Faithful

FINISHED

The truth of our tragedy is that
we never relieved each other's sadness
or found a way to quiet nervous nights
when ghosts of our pasts haunted dreams.

You lay on the couch, a burning cigarette
in your hand, and I found a quiet way
to slip it from your fingers before fire
reduced our unfulfilled lives to ash.
I lay down beside you, a fully clothed
lover with my hand across your chest
and over your heart. It was a romantic
dream to feel our warmth combined.
When you awoke, you turned your thin
face to me and smiled before you spoke
in words too soft to hear, but the sound
of your voice embraced my ears without
a conviction of love.

When we arose from the couch, we stood
face to face, no anticipated kiss, no
further nearness. You wanted another
cigarette, shrugged on your coat, and
headed out the back door to the patio.
You steamed the air with winter breath,

snapped a match on the brick wall
behind you and inhaled indifference..
My loneliness followed you. Darkness
kept you from seeing disappointment.
Your matter-of-fact shadow turned away
and finished the cigarette. We reentered
the house together, and you kept your coat
on ready to be driven home and away from
an evening that canceled commitment, an
evening of incremental goodbyes

RELINQUISHMENT

A surgeon has cut into my heart twice, and I felt nothing but the complexity of recovery. Being in love with you damaged my heart in a different way. Surgery cannot remove your unique walk, the way you leaned against a window full of late afternoon sun. Most days I ache with solemn remembrance and need a wizard to take away sadness. I walk, I ride a bike while looking back at seeing you introduce yourself after a thumbs up from across the bar room. You found your way into my summer and two thereafter. Our bodies rendered their narratives. We both seemed to have found a simple solution to loneliness, but then I discovered your deceptions and penchant for lies.

Since then, I've attempted to remove you from my mind, to write the final poem that frees me, but you hover in my heart. Many days I catch myself refusing to let you drift into oblivion. Some of your belongings are still stored in my shed, and occasionally when I look at them, I lift your sweatshirt simply to touch.

THE GHOST OF OLD LOVE COMES BACK ON SUNDAY

Somewhere deep in my childhood memories,
Sunday depressed me because the world shut
down except for movie theaters and gas stations,
and I endured day-long routines of Dad's face
in the newspaper and Mom clattering around
in the kitchen. All the while, I maneuvered
plastic soldiers in front of the Philco radio.

Today, however, I pace the floor, think
of the living, the dead, and you. I have
plastered my memory with images
of your youthful face, the April we walked
through Schiller Park, took snapshots of each
other.

Sunday is a graveyard of hymns to the past,
to recollections of infidelity when I walked
into your bedroom and saw deception
under the covers with you. Outside, ice
and snow finished December, and I escaped
into the worst weather possible, drove away
in a car that didn't seem to move. I wore a
noose home, chocking on the end of our
relationship.

Have I complained about Sunday? I would
take it to the dump if I could. And you?
I would like to bundle you in a permanent
goodbye and throw you away with the rest
of my remaining Sundays.

PERSONAL CONFETTI

It is August, one more month put away into the pocket of summer. If I could reshuffle months, I would return to June, toss out our bickering, have you lie down beside me before all is lost and pronounce solutions to the million mistakes that accompany sufficient love.

The bed we slept in is gone in a cloud of repression. Pettiness won. What was the point of constant analysis that would eventually kill our relationship?

I miss your warmth, the sweet smell of your neck, dawn when we awoke too early. My pen only touches on how much I miss you, your penchant for the color black, your desire to throw your past overboard like flotsam and jetsam.

I'm the one who tromped the brake down to the floorboards on our connection. Now, I suffer the ache of loss as it stretches from day to day. It's Sunday night, and I toss pieces of emotion onto paper like personal confetti when there is nothing left of us to celebrate.

BEGINNING AND CONCLUSION

> *...that*
> *perfect*
> *beginning and*
> *conclusion of our own...*
>
> from *The Sea*
> by Mary Oliver

I hear a train in the distance, its whistle
a subtle message of loneliness. Chills
of memory stumble across me like
a sudden curtain of cold. I could not
feel less for you than I do, but if my mind
turns in the wrong direction at the right time,
I remember ducks swimming in circles
on the pond in Schiller Park, a bystander
watching our hands touch, twilight sun flaming
petals of azaleas and rhododendrons.

I know you didn't understand the breakup
or the damage we'd done to one another.
There was a kind of inward bleeding
as if I'd wrapped our failure around a
sticky cactus, and I'm by myself again
listening to train whistles and letting
the moon rise without consequence. I am

back to not hearing your voice and not
centering the day around you. I know
how to stop the song of you by walking
into a room and feeling lucky for not finding
you there. Down the road and far into
the nostalgic night, the train is still whistling
as if it will take a lifetime for it to pass.

AFTERMATH

My legs are bowed from straddling defeat.
I still literally say your name in the quiet
hours of the night to heaven knows whom.

Have you grown into a new romance,
gone about your life convinced I didn't
care enough to prove otherwise? If I
would rent a cottage and lift you into
it bodily, would there be fewer questions
about our friendship and more serious
satisfaction than we thought possible?
By the log fire would we warm the
joy of being together?

All day I think of dropping deep into your
arms, my breath a slow dance to your kiss.

Perhaps it's meant to end. There would be
no surprise if you went away forever, made
of us a blackness like a house without windows.

I long for the late summer again when we met,
before whatever happiness we had became
a tug of war.

What happened that began the end?

My heart craves your hand in mine, the return
to steadfast promise.

THE PROGRESSION OF LETTING GO

All day I keep closing a mental door
on images of you. No sooner does one
disappear than another catches my
attention. I become brainwashed by
a gallery of the past, distraught that
I allow any kind of connection
to you. We fiercely fail each other,
yet I browse through pictures of
deception, snapshots of deceit. I
allow myself to long for anything
left of our relationship. I know I am
asking for two hands full of sorrow,
a reunion with distress, but I want
anything that doesn't include an end.

By late evening I stand by a window,
gaze at snow covered lawn, pick
around in my head for remnants of you.
A little time and darkness sobers me,
and I shut the door on remembrance.

In my dreams that night art and life
merge, and I surface as a man
looking for an uncomplicated romance,
arms holding me until I have to squint
to see the bad part of love.

FINALE

Obsessive persistence fills my brain
like oxygen fills lungs. Loving
you is a compulsive habit
like letting the cat in, tying a shoe,
clipping fingernails.

I stare at your needs like bare bulbs
that burn my eyes. In the mirror
under the ceiling light I see how
I have aged from paying the price
of being the man in your arms.
I know it is time to push you away
for more than awhile.

I want to talk about permanent
separation from the small box
that holds our lives, the limited
breathing space we call love.
Words can go on and on without
resolution. I want to make a poem
that prevents me from going back
into the fire again.

I am bloody and broken from battling
the results of your background. I press
my fist against my mouth to stifle
hysteria. I want to spit out that this
is the end, that I am here but cannot
help you anymore. This is my hand.
Do not take it.

THE ACT OF LEAVING

The unmistakable end of an affair,
when I carry my heart away
from the wreck, appears slow as a sunrise
one morning when I lift the blind and look
out the window at good-bye. I think
of black moments that made no sense.

You entered my life delicate as a
hand-painted saint, a ceramic representation
of innocence. Soon afterward, clay began
to crack, glaze discolor, and I studied
the real surface to find a lifelong habit
of substance abuse. I watched you slowly
rip your existence to shreds of ruined paper.

You huddled in the corner of excuses,
your brow heavy with frowns when I leaned
on you for truth. You inhabited a world
of door to door crime, holding hands behind
my back with homeboy miscreants.

Every day I moved ahead of your
devious machinations, your hobbled
together explanations until I hauled
presumptions and lies into the light.

At the window I let sun lock me in
its orange stare, the flaming room an exit
from a mismatch.

THE FINAL ACT OF LEAVING

You are gone and I am singing.

You said you would not return from your
undisclosed destination, and though I am
empty from your leaving and though I look
at snapshots of you, I will not soften into
regret that you are gone. Still,

I alternate between slipping into nostalgic
longing for your return and relief that the
relationship lies behind me. I know not
to grieve more than a little. I shudder at
time wasted trying to outguess lies, unable
to trust your alleged truths. Yes,

we once ambled under pink grandeur of
April blossoms, spent part of an October
afternoon on a bench watching a photographer
compose a wedding picture, but memories will
recede and fade like stories we heard as a child.
Eventually, we felt the strain of losing a mutual
bond, the heart's twinge that told us we would
separate.

I am sad but joyous now to awaken each
morning without the prospect of your calls
and texts. I enter the day more alive,
unmuddled by the south-of-the-tracks way
you lived and your deceptions, Today

I know I have to let go of you, lay aside second
guesses. I have finished watching you ruin your
life with drugs and no measure of self-pity. Today,

I hang out an exit sign.

DAMNED BY THE DECISION

I let you go. You vanished in black t-shirt,
paratrooper pants, and shoes just polished.

I stamped us finished, an inward verdict,
but outward my arms are full of emptiness.

When looking into the face of memory,
I see your eyes, green as variscite, skin
soft as plush. A pall paralyzes reason,
and I allow these thoughts that mitigate
the mockery we made of romance.

Our chance meeting misfired, led us
to think more existed between us than
reciprocal attraction. We trusted too
much to the selves we masqueraded as.

Since then, mutual manipulation has
made us mutilate tenderness, muster
a million criticisms that have
mushroomed into emotional murder.

You noticed me sitting in a bar, and
your nod negotiated a one-night stand
that should have been nipped in its
earliest hour.

Now, I narrate the loss, nurse the ache
I have caused in myself trying not to
need the narcotic I have made of you.

LAMENTING LOSS

You gone from my life is like bare walls
without mirrors or pictures. I manipulate
hours with the magnification of minor
tasks. I've mismanaged the outside, failed
for weeks to water hydrangea and hosta,
haven't bought a new garden hose. I didn't
manufacture reasons to abandon you.
They were apparent and already in place
before we met. I meander around the house.
I mope a little, murder myself with guilt.
I diverted you into other arms. The vacancy
swallows me as the deepest vortex would,
but I couldn't veneer your villainous acts:
stealing, forging checks, peddling dope.
I don't want you back. I shut the door,
trying to rework my life. Like Bartleby,
the Scrivener, I prefer not to think of you.
I am drunk with desire to believe
we never loved.

THE REALITY OF RETROSPECTION

I am wondering who you might be with.
Since I left you adrift, have you embraced
a new lover? I'm on a bench at Buckeye
Lake. Sky is cornflower blue, cloudless.
The afternoon sun is a deep yellow like
a black-eyed susan. The thought of you
is ebbing, but still flows through my mind,
unsatisfying.

Ducks dip their beaks for bread. Do they drift
in and out of relationships like people
or stay content with one another?
I know you well, body, habits, smell. Now
someone else will learn those things about you.
Maybe your lover already has. Sure I miss you,
not the drama, but deliberate demonstrations
of desire, doting the top of your head
with kisses, drawing you to me in an embrace.
It humiliates me to think I gave you
to someone else, but we wailed at one another
and never were at peace.

A distant fisherman on a rock pulls in a fish
I can't identify. I imagine him happy with it,
intending to keep the fish and not throw it back
for someone else to catch.

CONCLUSION

No one will want you again the way I did.
I was the man with flowers in my hand,
someone who wanted to start life again,
pleaded with a past to let me go
forward. Your world is behind me
like a sun disappearing in a rearview
mirror. A thousand hours of texting
did not fix our fractured relationship.
Letting you go was my salvation.
I've found the rest of me, the small
part I didn't give away. Whatever
happened between us is a myth,
a moment when the bow of the boat
looked like it had a direction. We
met as a result of randomness,
two people in a room disappearing
into the possibility of the other. Our
affinity was unplanned and unfortunate.
You filched the finest part of me,
flipped it into the gutter like
a cigarette butt. I'm finally finished
being hungry for you, offering
myself a very substantial end.

EMPTY STREETS

All through the four years we were partners
I didn't know how edgy mistrust could make
me.

In the beginning I had no clue about your
addiction to pills and heroin. I'm lucky
to have escaped from the alleys that you
dragged me through for a fix I drove you
to houses with boarded windows and
guarded doors. I hadn't intended to assume
the role of an enabler, but in trying to flee
my empty life I got caught up in yours, and
before I knew it, I was in over my head.

I was completely sold on the story
of your parents introducing you to
drugs as a child and tried to undo the
damage they had done by offering you
personal goals, perpetual help. I failed
to counterbalance the corrosion of
your youth.

I yearned to learn how to love you,
someone who practically made a home
of the streets, but I failed also in assuming
I could ultimately make a difference.

In the end you slung ugly words at me
as if they were clinched fists, ignored
my last effort to offer affection. We
had tired of the ungentle arguments.
It was time for me to admit defeat
and to let you find love elsewhere.

EPILOGUE

The all-day downpour pools around tree trunks.
From the window I watch rain against the glare
of gray sky. The refrigerator purrs. Otherwise,
the house is an abandoned quiet.

Today a chill spirals down into my stomach,
and I celebrate the end of a relationship
by pinning a corsage of finality to the naked
skin of my heart. You have been insulting and
abusive, engulfing me with four years of criminal
activity and infidelity. All I can do is look
at the chairs, the table, the couch
and feel humiliated by my sorrow and
gluttonous desire to resolve our differences and
start again. You took from me and never gave,
yet I despair that you will probably not return to me.
Why should I want to resume a relationship that
has deteriorated into profound meanness?
I walk around the house wanting the sight of you
in my life again. Such deep longing is a sickness
beyond prayer. Truly, I want to be free
of what is dead, untrapped from the interminable
dread that I have lost you for good.

All around me the furniture stares, mute reminders of where we stood and sat. I will never be satisfied until I overcome the loss of you, until I can look out on a rainy day and not be filled with remorse and the ragged whisper in my ear of what could have been happiness.

Dr. R. Nikolas Macioci earned a PhD from The Ohio State University and taught English, Writers' Seminar (a course he created for select students), and Drama in Columbus City Schools. OCTELA, the Ohio Council of Teachers of English, awarded Nik Macioci best secondary English teacher in the state of Ohio.

He won First Place in the 1987 National Writer's Union Poetry Competition judged by Denise Levertov, First Place in The Baudelaire Award Competition sponsored by The World Order of Narrative and Formalist Poets (1989). Second Place in Zone 3's first annual Rainmaker Awards, judged by Howard Nemerov (1989), and Second Place in the Writer's Digest annual competition, Judged by Diane Wakoski (1991).

Nik is the author of two chapbooks, *Cafes of Childhood,* and *Greatest Hits*, as well as five books: *Cafes of Childhood* (the original chapbook with additional poems), *Why Dance?, Necessary Windows, Mother Goosed* and *Occasional Heaven.* Forth-coming is *Rough.* His book, *Cafes of Childhood* was submitted for the Pulitzer Prize. Critics and judges called *Cafes of Childhood* a "beautifully harrowing account of child abuse, but not "sentimental" or self-pitying" an "amazing book," and "a single unified whole." In addition, Nik's work has been published in more than two hundred magazines here and abroad. Most recently, Macioci has published in *The Society of Classical Poets journal, Clark Street Review, Blue Unicorn,* and *Chiron Review.* He is a member of Bistro poets critique group.

www.ingramcontent.com/pod-product-compliance
Lightning Source LLC
Chambersburg PA
CBHW030121100526
44591CB00009B/484